CATHOLIC NOVENAS

Edited by
Bart Tesoriero

Library of Congress Control Number: 2011910837
ISBN 1-936020-44-7

Artwork ©2002 Ambrosiana, Phoenix, Arizona
Text ©2002 Autom, Phoenix, Arizona
Eleventh Printing, November 2011

What is a Novena?

Before His ascension into heaven, Jesus directed His apostles to wait and pray for the coming of the Holy Spirit. With Mary, they prayed in Jerusalem for nine days. The next morning, Pentecost, they were all filled with the Holy Spirit and the Church was born. In later years, the practice of praying nine days for a special intention developed. This devotion was called a novena, from the Latin word for nine: *novem*. A novena, then, refers to devotions which take place over nine consecutive days or, in some cases, one day a week over nine consecutive weeks.

Through the many novenas prayed down the long ages of the Church, believers have sought for and found help, relief, and peace from God. **Catholic Novenas** includes fifteen of the Church's most beloved novenas.

Jesus told us, "Therefore I tell you, all that you ask for in prayer, believe that you will receive and it shall be yours." We encourage you to pray these novenas with faith in a loving Father who cares for you and is working out His Will in your life.

Table of Contents

Novena to the Sacred Heart of Jesus 5

Novena to Saint Joseph 15

Novena to Saint Anthony 23

Novena to Saint Theresa 29

Novena to Saint Jude 37

Novena to the Infant of Prague 43

Novena to Saint Gerard 49

Novena to the Holy Spirit 55

Novena to Our Lady of Perpetual Help 63

Novena to Saint Peregrine 67

Novena to Our Lady of the Miraculous Medal 71

Novena to Saint Dymphna 75

Novena to Our Lady of Mt. Carmel 77

Novena to Saint Rita 83

Novena to Saint Anne 87

First Day

Act of Consecration to the Most Sacred Heart of Jesus

Pray every day for nine days:

O most loving Jesus, Redeemer of the human race, behold us humbly prostrate before Your altar. We are Yours and Yours we wish to be. But to be more surely united to You, behold each one of us freely consecrates himself today to Your most Sacred Heart. Many, indeed, have never known You, many, too, despising Your precepts, have rejected You. Have mercy on them all, most merciful Jesus, and draw them to Your Sacred Heart.

Be King, O Lord, not only of the faithful who have never forsaken You, but also of the prodigal children who have abandoned You. Grant that they may quickly return to their Father' house, lest they die of wretchedness and hunger.

Be King of all those who are still involved in the darkness of idolatry, whom discord keeps aloof, and call them back to the harbor of truth and unity of faith, so that soon there may be but one flock and one Shepherd.

Grant, O Lord, to Your Church, assurance of freedom and immunity from harm, Give peace and order to all nations. Make the earth resound from pole to pole with one cry, "Praise to the divine Heart that wrought our salvation. To It be glory and honor forever."

Amen.

Each day add the appropriate prayer as shown.

Second Day

Novena Prayer

Divine Jesus, You have said, "Ask and you shall receive; seek and you shall find; knock and it shall be opened to you." Behold me kneeling at Your feet, filled with a lively faith and confidence in the promises of Your Sacred Heart. I come to ask this favor: *(Mention your request.)*

To whom can I turn if not to You, Whose Heart is the source of all graces and merits? Where should I seek if not in the treasure which contains all the riches of Your kindness and mercy? Where should I knock if not at the door through which God gives Himself to us and through which we go to God?

I have recourse to You, Heart of Jesus. In You I find consolation, protection, strength, and light. Dear Jesus, I firmly believe You can grant me the grace I implore, even should it require a miracle. You have only to will it and my prayer will be granted. I admit I am most unworthy of Your favors, but this is not a reason for me to be discouraged. You are the God of mercies, and You will not refuse a contrite heart. Cast upon me a look of mercy, I beg of You, and Your kind Heart will find in my miseries and weakness a reason for granting my prayer.

Sacred Heart, whatever may be Your decision, I will never stop adoring, loving, praising, and serving You. I resign myself, O Lord, to Your Will, which I sincerely desire may be fulfilled in all Your creatures forever. Grant me this grace through the Immaculate Heart of Your most sorrowful Mother. Amen.

Third Day

I. O my Jesus, You have said: "Truly I say to you, ask and you will receive, seek and you will find, knock and it will be opened to you." Behold I knock, I seek and ask for the grace of *(here name your request)*.

Our Father, Hail Mary, Glory Be to the Father. **Sacred Heart of Jesus, I place all my trust in You.**

II. O my Jesus, You have said: "Truly I say to you, if you ask anything of the Father in my name, he will give it to you." Behold, in Your name, I ask the Father for the grace of *(here name your request)*.

Our Father, Hail Mary, Glory Be to the Father. **Sacred Heart of Jesus, I place all my trust in You.**

III. O my Jesus, You have said: "Truly I say to you, heaven and earth will pass away but my words will not pass away." Encouraged by Your infallible words I now ask for the grace of *(here name your request)*.

Our Father, Hail Mary, Glory Be to the Father. **Sacred Heart of Jesus, I place all my trust in You.**

O Sacred Heart of Jesus, for whom it is impossible not to have compassion on the afflicted, have pity on us miserable sinners and grant us the grace which we ask of You, through the Sorrowful and Immaculate Heart of Mary, Your tender Mother and ours.

***Pray the Hail, Holy Queen and add:* Saint Joseph, foster father of Jesus, pray for us.** – *Saint Margaret Mary Alacoque*

(This novena prayer was recited by Padre Pio every day)

Fourth Day

Today, meditate on the **Twelve Promises** of Jesus to Saint Margaret Mary telling her how He would help those who honor His Sacred Heart:

1. I will give them all the graces necessary for their state of life.

2. I will give peace in their families.

3. I will console them in all their troubles.

4. They shall find in My Heart an assured refuge during life and especially at the hour of death.

5. I will pour abundant blessings on all their undertakings.

6. Sinners shall find in My Heart the source and infinite ocean of mercy.

7. Tepid souls shall become fervent.

8. Fervent souls shall speedily rise to great perfection.

9. I will bless the homes in which the image of My Sacred Heart shall be exposed and honored.

10. I will give to priests the power to touch the most hardened hearts.

11. Those who propagate this devotion shall have their name written in My Heart, and it shall never be effaced.

12. The all-powerful love of My Heart will grant to all those who shall receive Communion on the First Friday of nine consecutive months the grace of final repentance; they shall not die under My displeasure, nor without receiving their Sacraments; My Heart shall be their assured refuge at that last hour.

Fifth Day

Consecration of the Family to the Sacred Heart of Jesus

Sacred Heart of Jesus, You desire to be King in Christian families.

Today we proclaim Your most complete kingly dominion over our own family. We want to live with Your life. We want Your virtues to flourish in our home. We want to banish far from us the spirit of darkness.

You shall be King over our minds in the simplicity of our faith, and over our hearts by the wholehearted love with which they shall burn for You, the flame of which we will keep alive by the frequent reception of Your Divine Eucharist.

Please preside, O Divine Heart, over our gatherings; bless our enterprises, both spiritual and temporal; dispel our cares, sanctify our joys, and alleviate our sufferings. Should we ever have the misfortune to afflict You, remind us, O Heart of Jesus, that You are good and merciful to the penitent sinner. And when the hour of separation strikes, when death comes into our midst, help us to accept Your eternal decrees.

We shall console ourselves with the thought that someday our entire family, reunited in heaven, will sing forever Your glories and Your mercies. May the Immaculate Heart of Mary and the glorious patriarch Saint Joseph present this consecration to You, and keep it in our minds all the days of our life. All glory to the Heart of Jesus, our King and our Father!

Sixth Day

NOVENA PRAYERS TO THE SACRED HEART

O Most Holy Heart of Jesus, fountain of every blessing, I adore You, I love You, and with a lively sorrow for my sins, I offer You this poor heart of mine. Make me humble, patient and pure, and wholly obedient to Your Will. Grant, good Jesus, that I may live in You, and for You. Protect me in danger, comfort me in afflictions, give health of body, assistance in temporal needs, Your blessing on all that I do, and the grace of a holy death.

O Sacred Heart of Jesus, I come to You, throwing myself into the arms of Your tender mercy. You are my sure refuge, my unfailing and only hope. You are the remedy for all my evils, relief for all my miseries, and reparation for all my faults. You can supply what is wanting in me in order to obtain fully the graces that I ask for myself and others. You are for us all, the infallible, inexhaustible source of light, strength, perseverance, peace and consolation. I am certain that my persistence will never weary You; certain, too, that You will never cease to aid, protect, and love me, because Your love for me, O Divine Heart, is infinite. Have mercy on me then, O Heart of Jesus, and on all that I recommend to You, according to Your own mercy, and do with us, for us, and in us, whatsoever You will, for we abandon ourselves to You with the full, entire confidence and conviction that You will never abandon us either in time or eternity. Amen.

Seventh Day

Prayer to the Sacred Heart for the Hour of Death

O Sacred Heart of Jesus, mercifully accept the prayer which I now make to You for help in the moment of my death, when at its approach all my senses shall fail me.

When, therefore, O kind and merciful Jesus, my weary and downcast eyes can no longer look up to You, be mindful of the loving gaze which I now turn to You, and have mercy on me, a sinner.

When my lips can no longer kiss Your most sacred wounds, remember those kisses which I now give You, and have mercy on me, a sinner.

When my hands can no longer embrace Your cross, forget not the affection with which I embrace it now, and have mercy upon me, a sinner.

When my tongue can no longer speak, remember that I called upon You now. Jesus, Mary, and Joseph; to you I commend my soul. O Sacred Heart of Jesus, filled with infinite love, accept this act of consecration that I make to You of all that I am and all that I have.

Take every part of me, and draw me day by day nearer to Your Sacred Heart. There, as I can bear the lesson, teach me Your blessed way.

O Sacred Heart of Jesus, I entreat You, in the hour of my death say to Your divine Father, "Father forgive him (her)"; Say to my soul, "This day you shall be with Me in Paradise."

O Queen of the Holy Rosary, pray for us. Amen. *(One Our Father, Hail Mary, and Glory Be to the Father.)*

Eighth Day

Prayer for the Forgiveness of Daily Neglects

Eternal Father, I offer the Sacred Heart of Jesus with all Its love, all Its sufferings and all Its merits:

First - to expiate all the sins I have committed this day and during all my life. (Glory Be)

Second - to purify the good I have done badly this day and during all my life. (Glory Be.)

Third - to supply for the good I ought to have done and I have neglected this day and during all my life. (Glory Be.)

O Sacred Heart of Jesus, I Place My Trust in Thee

O Sacred Heart of Jesus, I place my trust in Thee, Whatever may befall me, Lord, though dark the hour may be;

In all my woes, in all my joys, though naught but grief I see,

O Sacred Heart of Jesus, I place my trust in Thee.

When those I loved have passed away, and I am sore distressed,

O Sacred Heart of Jesus, I fly to Thee for rest.

In all my trials, great or small, my confidence shall be

Unshaken as I cry, dear Lord, I place my trust in Thee.

This is my one sweet prayer, dear Lord, my faith, my trust, my love,

But most of all in that last hour, when death points up above,

O sweet Savior, may Thy face smile on my soul all free;

Oh may I cry with rapturous love: "I've placed my trust in Thee!"

Ninth Day

Prayer to the Sacred Heart for Priests

Remember, O most loving Heart of Jesus, that they for whom I pray are those for whom You prayed so earnestly the night before Your death. These are they to whom You look to continue with You in Your sorrows when others forsake You, who share Your griefs and have inherited your persecutions, according to Your Word: "The servant is not greater than his Lord". Remember, O Heart of Jesus, that Your priests are the objects of the world's hatred and Satan's deadliest snares. Keep them then, O Jesus, in the safe citadel of Your Sacred Heart and there let them be sanctified in truth. May they be one with you and one among themselves, and grant that multitudes may be brought through their word to believe in You and love You. Amen.

Prayer to the Eternal Father

"O Eternal Father, through the divine Heart of Jesus, I adore You for all those who adore You not; I love You for all those who do not love You. I go in spirit through the whole world to seek for souls redeemed by the blood of Jesus. I embrace them in order to present them to You in His Sacred Heart, and in union with Your merciful Heart, I ask for their conversion."

– *Blessed Marie of the Incarnation*

"Jesus is the only true friend of our hearts."

– *Saint Margaret Mary*

Novena Prayer to Saint Joseph
over 1900 years old

*Say for nine consecutive mornings for anything you may desire.
It has seldom been known to fail.*

O Saint Joseph whose protection is so great, so strong, so prompt before the Throne of God, I place in you all my interests and desires.

O Saint Joseph, do assist me by your powerful intercession and obtain for me from your Divine Son all spiritual blessings through Jesus Christ, Our Lord; so that having engaged here below your Heavenly power I may offer my thanksgiving and homage to the most Loving of Fathers. O Saint Joseph, I never weary contemplating you and Jesus asleep in your arms. I dare not approach while He reposes near your heart. Press Him in my name and kiss His fine Head for me, and ask Him to return the Kiss when I draw my dying breath. Saint Joseph, Patron of departing souls, pray for us. Amen.

This prayer was found in the fiftieth year of Our Lord Jesus Christ. In the 1500s it was sent by the Pope to Emperor Charles when he was going into battle. Whoever reads this prayer, hears it or carries it, will never die a sudden death, nor be drowned, nor will poison take effect on them. They will not fall into the hands of the enemy nor be burned in any fire, nor will they be defeated in battle.

First Day

Foster Father of Jesus

Saint Joseph, you were privileged to share in the mystery of the Incarnation as the foster-father of Jesus. You helped to protect Mary's virginity before and during your married life with her.

You shared in the support, upbringing, and protection of the Divine Child as His foster father. For this purpose the Heavenly Father gave you the genuine heart of a father — a heart full of love and self-sacrifice.

Dear Saint Joseph, help us also to fulfill God's Will in our lives by cooperating as closely as we can with the graces and blessings Our Lord sends us every day. May His Kingdom come!

Second Day

Virginal Husband of Mary

Saint Joseph, I honor you as the true husband of Mary, who belonged to you with all she was and had. No other person so won her esteem, obedience, and love.

This union of marriage brought you into daily familiar association with Mary, the loveliest of God's creatures, and enabled you to share with her a mutual spirituality. Mary found her edification in your calm, humble, and deep virtue, purity, and sanctity. Your marriage was the way in which God chose to have Jesus introduced into the world, a great divine mystery from which all benefits have come to us.

Saint Joseph, I thank God for your privilege of being the virginal husband of Mary. I beg of you to obtain for me the grace to love Jesus with all my heart, as you did, and to love Mary with some of the tenderness and loyalty with which you loved her.

Third Day

Man Chosen by the Blessed Trinity

Saint Joseph, God the Father granted you all the graces and blessings you needed to be His chosen representative on earth.

Desirous of a worthy foster father, God the Son chose you, adding His own riches and gifts, and above all, His love. The true measure of your sanctity is to be judged by your imitation of Jesus. You were entirely consecrated to Jesus, working always near Him, offering Him your virtues, your work, your sufferings, your very life. Jesus lived in you so perfectly that you were transformed into Him. Hence, after Mary, you are the holiest of the saints.

You were chosen by the Holy Spirit. Every vocation and every fulfillment of a vocation proceeds from the Holy Spirit. As foster father of Jesus and head of the Holy Family, you had an exalted and most responsible vocation — to open the way for the redemption of the world and to prepare for it by the education and guidance of Jesus. In this work the Holy Spirit was the guide; you obeyed and carried out the works. How perfectly you obeyed God's guidance!

Saint Joseph, I thank God for choosing you. Please obtain for me the grace to imitate your virtues so that I too may be pleasing to the Heart of God. Help me to give myself entirely to His service and to the accomplishment of His Holy Will, that one day I may reach heaven and be eternally united to God as you are.

Fourth Day

Faithful Servant

Saint Joseph, you lived for one purpose — to be the personal servant of Jesus Christ, the Word made flesh. You were at the same time the foster father of Jesus, and His disciple as well.

Every moment of your life was consecrated to the service of our Lord: sleep, rest, work, pain. Faithful to your duties, you sacrificed everything unselfishly, even cheerfully.

Saint Joseph, please obtain for me the grace to be a faithful servant of God as you were. Help me to share in your obedience, to trust in God's Will, and to be calm in my trials. Help me imitate your generosity, for there can be no greater reward here on earth than the joy and honor of being a faithful servant of God.

Fifth Day

Patron of the Church

Saint Joseph, God has appointed you patron of the Catholic Church because you were the father, protector, guide and support of the Holy Family, the starting-point of the Church, God's family on earth. You have a special relationship to the priesthood because you reared Jesus. You supported, nourished, protected and sheltered our Savior Himself.

Saint Joseph, please obtain for me the grace to live always as a worthy member of the Church, so that through it I may save my soul.

Through your powerful intercession may the Church successfully accomplish its mission in this world — the glory of God and the salvation of souls!

Sixth Day

Patron of Families

Saint Joseph, I venerate you as the gentle head of the Holy Family. You lived, moved, and acted in the loving company of Jesus and Mary, and even died in their arms. Your family life at Nazareth radiated divine charity. Jesus chose to fulfill toward you all the duties of a faithful son, showing you every mark of honor and affection due to a parent, and Mary loved you as a devoted wife.

You responded to this love and veneration with the deepest love and respect. You had for Jesus a true fatherly love, and your love for Mary grew stronger every day.

God has made you the patron of family life because of how peacefully and happily the Holy Family rested under the care of your fatherly rule. You are the patron and intercessor of families, and you deserve a place in every home.

Saint Joseph, please obtain God's blessing upon my own family. Make our home and the home of each Christian family the kingdom of Jesus and Mary – a kingdom of peace, of joy, and love.

Grant that we may be reunited in God's Kingdom and eternally live in the company of the Holy Family in heaven.

Seventh Day

Patron of Workers

Saint Joseph, God willed that you and your foster Son should spend your days together working as carpenters. What a beautiful example you set for the working classes! It was especially for the poor that Jesus came upon earth. Jesus Himself ennobled labor by freely embracing it. Thus He teaches us that for the humbler class of workmen, He has in store His richest graces, provided they live content in the place God's Providence has assigned them, and remain poor in spirit.

From the Divine Master, who worked along with you, you learned to work in the presence of God in the spirit of prayer, for as He worked He adored His Father and recommended the welfare of the world to Him.

Saint Joseph, please obtain for me the grace to respect the dignity of labor and to be content with my position in life, however lowly, where God has placed me. Teach me to work for God and with God in the spirit of humility and prayer, as you did, so that I may offer my toil in union with the sacrifice of Jesus in the Mass as a reparation for my sins, and gain rich merit for heaven.

Eighth Day

Friend in Suffering

Saint Joseph, all the mysteries of Jesus' life were more or less mysteries of suffering, and you shared in many of them. You endured suffering in the uncertainty regarding Mary's virginity, in the prophecy of Simeon, the flight into Egypt, and the loss of Jesus in the Temple. You were surely burdened by the sins of your own people.

You bore all this suffering in a truly Christ-like manner, silently and cheerfully, knowing well that true love is a crucified love. But God never forsook you in your trials. The trials, too, disappeared and were changed at last into consolation and joy.

God allowed your life to be filled with suffering as well as consolation to remind us that all of life is a matter of dying and rising. Teach me to gratefully accept whatever He sends me, and during the time of consolation to prepare for suffering.

Dear Saint Joseph, many have turned to you in distress and have always found in you a faithful friend. Please grant that I may unite my sufferings, works, and disappointments with Jesus and Mary, and offer them to God, who makes all things work together for the good.

Ninth Day

Patron of a Happy Death

Saint Joseph, how fitting it was at your death that Jesus should stand at your bedside with Mary, the sweetness and hope of all mankind.

You gave your entire life to the service of Jesus and Mary; at death you enjoyed the consolation of dying in their loving arms. You accepted death in the spirit of loving submission to the Will of God, and this acceptance crowned your hidden life of virtue. Yours was a merciful judgment, for your foster Son was your Judge, and Mary was your advocate.

You looked into eternity and to your everlasting reward with confidence. If our Savior blessed the shepherds, the Magi, Simeon, John the Baptist, and others, because they devotedly greeted Him for a brief passing hour, how much more did He bless you, His foster father? Our Divine Savior paid His debt of gratitude by granting you many graces in your lifetime, and the final grace of a peaceful death.

Saint Joseph, please obtain for me also the grace of a happy death. Help me to remember daily my final end, and to accept death in the spirit of resignation to God's Holy Will. May I die, as you did, in the arms of Jesus, strengthened by Holy Viaticum, and in the arms of Mary, with her rosary in my hand and her name on my lips!

Novena to Saint Anthony of Padua

Pray daily:

O wonderful Saint Anthony, glorious on account of the fame of your miracles, and through the condescension of Jesus in coming in the form of a little child to rest in your arms, obtain for me of His bounty the grace which I ardently desire from the depths of my heart . . . You who were so compassionate toward miserable sinners, regard not the unworthiness of those who pray to you, but the glory of God that it may once again be magnified by the granting of the particular request ... which I now ask for with persevering earnestness. Amen.

One Our Father, one Hail Mary, and Glory Be to the Father, in honor of Saint Anthony. Saint Anthony, pray for us!

First Day

O holy Saint Anthony, gentlest of saints, your love for God and charity for his creatures made you worthy while on earth to possess miraculous powers. Miracles awaited your word, which you were ever ready to speak for those in trouble or anxiety. Encouraged by this thought, I implore you to obtain for me the favor I seek in this novena (*mention your request*). The answer to my prayer may require a miracle; even so, you are the saint of miracles. O gentle and loving Saint Anthony, whose heart was ever full of human sympathy, whisper my petition into the ears of the Infant Jesus, who loved to be folded in your arms, and the gratitude of my heart will always be yours.

One Our Father, one Hail Mary, and Glory Be to the Father, in honor of Saint Anthony. Saint Anthony, pray for us!

Second Day

O miracle-working Saint Anthony, remember that it never has been heard that you left without help or relief anyone who in their need had recourse to you. Animated now with the most lively confidence, even with full conviction of not being refused, I fly for refuge to you, O most favored friend of the Infant Jesus. O eloquent preacher of the divine mercy, despise not my supplications but, bringing them before the throne of God, strengthen them by your intercession and obtain for me the favor I seek in this novena *(mention your request)*.

One Our Father, one Hail Mary, and Glory Be to the Father, in honor of Saint Anthony. Saint Anthony, pray for us!

Third Day

O purest Saint Anthony, through your angelic virtue you were made worthy to be caressed by the Divine Child Jesus, to hold Him in your arms and press Him to your heart. I entreat you to cast a benevolent glance upon me. O glorious Saint Anthony, born under the protection of Mary Immaculate on the Feast of her Assumption into Heaven, consecrated to her, and now so powerful an intercessor in Heaven, I beg you to obtain for me the favor I ask in this novena *(mention your request)*. O great wonder worker, intercede for me that God may grant my request.

One Our Father, one Hail Mary, and Glory Be to the Father, in honor of Saint Anthony. Saint Anthony, pray for us!

Fourth Day

I salute and honor you, O powerful helper, Saint Anthony. The Christian world confidently turns to you and experiences your tender compassion and powerful assistance in many necessities and sufferings. I am encouraged in my need to seek your help in obtaining a favorable answer to my request for the favor I seek in this novena *(mention your request)*. O holy Saint Anthony, I beg you, obtain for me the grace that I desire.

One Our Father, one Hail Mary, and Glory Be to the Father, in honor of Saint Anthony. Saint Anthony, pray for us!

Fifth Day

I salute you, Saint Anthony, lily of purity, ornament and glory of Christianity. I salute you, great Saint, cherub of wisdom and seraph of divine love. I rejoice at the favors our Lord has so liberally bestowed upon you. In humility and confidence I entreat you to help me, for I know that God has given you charity and pity, as well as power. I ask you by the love you felt toward the Infant Jesus as you held Him in your arms to tell Him now of the favor I seek through your intercession in this novena *(mention your request)*.

One Our Father, one Hail Mary, and Glory Be to the Father, in honor of Saint Anthony. Saint Anthony, pray for us!

Sixth Day

O glorious Saint Anthony, chosen by God to preach His Word, you received from Him the gift of tongues and the power of working the most extraordinary miracles. O good Saint Anthony, pray that I may fulfill the will of God in all things so that I may love Him, with you, for all eternity. O kind Saint Anthony, I beseech you, obtain for me the grace that I desire, the favor I seek in this novena *(mention your request)*.

One Our Father, one Hail Mary, and Glory Be to the Father, in honor of Saint Anthony. Saint Anthony, pray for us!

Seventh Day

O renowned champion of the faith of Christ, most holy Saint Anthony, glorious for your many miracles, obtain for me from the bounty of my Lord and God the grace which I ardently seek in this novena *(mention your request)*. O holy Saint Anthony, ever attentive to those who invoke you, grant me the aid of your powerful intercession.

One Our Father, one Hail Mary, and Glory Be to the Father, in honor of Saint Anthony. Saint Anthony, pray for us!

Eighth Day

O holy Saint Anthony, you have shown yourself so powerful in your intercession, so tender and so compassionate toward those who honor you and invoke you in suffering and distress. I beseech you most humbly and earnestly to take me under your protection in my present necessities and to obtain for me the favor I desire *(mention your request)*. Recommend my request to the merciful Queen of Heaven, that she may plead my cause with you before the throne of her Divine Son.

One Our Father, one Hail Mary, and Glory Be to the Father, in honor of Saint Anthony. Saint Anthony, pray for us!

Ninth Day

Saint Anthony, servant of Mary, glory of the Church, pray for our Holy Father, our bishops, our priests, our Religious Orders, that, through their pious zeal and apostolic labors, all may be united in faith and give greater glory to God. Saint Anthony, helper of all who invoke you, pray for me and intercede for me before the throne of Almighty God that I be granted the favor I so earnestly seek in this novena *(mention your request)*.

One Our Father, one Hail Mary, and Glory Be to the Father, in honor of Saint Anthony. Saint Anthony, pray for us!

May the divine assistance remain always with us. Amen.

May the souls of the faithful departed, through the mercy of God, rest in peace. Amen.

Little Flower Novena

Prayers to be said each day: Come Holy Spirit, fill the hearts of the faithful, and kindle in them the fire of Your divine love.

V. Send forth Your Spirit and they shall be created.

R. And You shall renew the face of the earth.

Let us pray: O God, who has instructed the hearts of the faithful by the light of the Holy Spirit; grant that by the gift of the same Spirit, we may be ever truly wise and rejoice in His consolation, through Christ our Lord. Amen.

Acts of Faith, Hope, and Love: O my God! I believe in Thee: strengthen my faith. All my hopes are in Thee: do Thou secure them. I love Thee: teach me to love Thee daily more and more.

The Act of Contrition: O my God! I am heartily sorry for having offended You, and I detest all my sins, because I dread the loss of heaven and the pains of hell, but most of all because they offend You, my God, who are all good and deserving of all my love. I firmly resolve, with the help of Your grace, to confess my sins, to do penance, and to amend my life. Amen.

Concluding Prayer Prayed Each Day: O Lord, You have said: "Unless you become as little children you shall not enter the kingdom of heaven." Grant us, we beg You, so to follow, in humility and simplicity of heart, the footsteps of the Virgin blessed Thérèse, that we may attain to an everlasting reward. Amen.

First Day

Saint Thérèse, privileged Little Flower of Jesus and Mary, I approach you with childlike confidence and deep humility. I lay before you my desires, and beg that through your intercession they may be realized. Did you not promise to spend your heaven doing good upon earth?

Grant me according to this promise the favors I am asking from you.

Intercede for us all the days of our life, but especially during this Novena and obtain for us from God the graces and favors we ask through your intercession. Amen.

Second Day

O dear little Saint, now that you see the crucified and risen Jesus in heaven, still bearing the wounds caused by sin, you know still more clearly than you did upon earth the value of souls, and the priceless worth of that Precious Blood which He shed to save them. As I am one of those children for whom Christ died, obtain for me all the graces I need in order to profit by that Precious Blood. Use your great power with our divine Lord and pray for me.

Intercede for us all the days of our life, but especially during this Novena and obtain for us from God the graces and favors we ask through your intercession. Amen.

Third Day

Dear Little Flower, make all things lead me to heaven and God. Whether I look at the sun, the moon, the stars and the vast expanse in which they float, or whether I look at the flowers of the field, the trees of the forest, the beauties of the earth so full of color and so glorious, may they speak to me of the love and power of God; may they all sing His praises in my ear. Like you, may I daily love Him more and more in return for His gifts. Teach me often to deny myself in my dealings with others, that I may offer to Jesus many little sacrifices.

Intercede for us all the days of our life, but especially during this Novena and obtain for us from God the graces and favors we ask through your intercession. Amen.

Fourth Day

Dear Little Flower of Carmel, bearing so patiently the disappointments and delays allowed by God, and preserving in the depths of your soul an unchanging peace because you sought only God's Will, ask for me complete conformity to that adorable Will in all the trials and disappointments of life. If the favors I am asking during this Novena are pleasing to God, obtain them for me. If not, it is true I shall feel the refusal keenly, but I too wish only God's Will, and pray in the words you used, that it "may ever be perfectly fulfilled in me."

Intercede for us all the days of our life, but especially during this Novena and obtain for us from God the graces and favors we ask through your intercession. Amen.

Fifth Day

Little Flower of Jesus, from the very first moment of your religious life you thought only of denying yourself in all things so as to follow Jesus more perfectly; help me to bear patiently the trials of my daily life.

Teach me to make use of the trials, the sufferings, the humiliations, that come my way, to learn to know myself better and to love God more.

Intercede for us all the days of our life, but especially during this Novena and obtain for us from God the graces and favors we ask through your intercession. Amen.

Sixth Day

Saint Thérèse, Patroness of the Missions, be a great missionary throughout the world to the end of time. Remind our Master of His own words, "The harvest is great, but the laborers are few." Your zeal for souls was so great; obtain a like zeal for those now working for souls, and beg God to multiply their numbers, that the millions to whom Jesus is yet unknown may be brought to know, love and follow Him.

Intercede for us all the days of our life, but especially during this Novena and obtain for us from God the graces and favors we ask through your intercession. Amen.

Seventh Day

O little martyr of Love, you know now even better than in the days of your pilgrimage that Love embraces all vocations; that it is love alone which counts, which unites us perfectly to God and conforms our will with His. All you sought on earth was love; to love Jesus as He had never yet been loved. Use your power in heaven to make us love Him. If only we love Him we shall desire to make Him loved by others; we shall pray much for souls. We shall no longer fear death, for it will unite us to Him forever. Obtain for us the grace to do all for the love of God, to give Him pleasure, to love Him so well that He may be pleased with us as He was with you.

Intercede for us all the days of our life, but especially during this Novena and obtain for us from God the graces and favors we ask through your intercession. Amen.

Eighth Day

Dear Saint Thérèse, like you I have to die one day. I beseech you, obtain from God, by reminding Him of your own precious death, that I may have a holy death, strengthened by the Sacraments of the Church, entirely resigned to the most holy Will of God, and burning with love for Him. May my last words on earth be, "My God, I love You."

Intercede for us all the days of our life, but especially during this Novena and obtain for us from God the graces and favors we ask through your intercession. Amen.

Ninth Day

Dear Little Saint Thérèse, by love and suffering while you were on earth, you won the power with God which you now enjoy in heaven. Since your life there began, you have showered down countless blessings on this poor world; you have been an instrument made use of by your divine Spouse to work countless miracles. I beg of you to remember all my wants. Sufferings must come to me also; may I use them to love God more, and follow my Jesus better. You are especially the little missionary of love. Make me love Jesus more, and all others for His sake. With all my heart I thank the most Holy Trinity for the wonderful blessings conferred on you, and upon the world through you.

Intercede for us all the days of our life, but especially during this Novena and obtain for us from God the graces and favors we ask through your intercession. Amen.

Novena to Saint Jude

To be prayed in cases despaired of

Daily Prayer to Saint Jude

Saint Jude, glorious apostle, faithful servant and friend of Jesus, the name of the traitor has caused you to be forgotten by many. However, the Church honors and invokes you universally as the patron of hopeless cases, and of things despaired of. Pray for me who am so distressed. Make use, I implore you, of that particular privilege accorded you to bring visible and speedy help where help was almost despaired of. Come to my assistance in this great need that I may receive the consolation and the aid of Heaven in all my necessities, tribulations, and sufferings, particularly *(mention your request)* and that I may bless God with you and all the elect throughout eternity. Saint Jude, apostle, martyr, and relative of our Lord Jesus Christ, of Mary, and of Joseph, intercede for us! Amen.

First Day

O blessed apostle Saint Jude, who labored zealously among the Gentiles in many lands, and performed numerous miracles in needy and despairing cases, we invoke you to take special interest in us and our needs. We feel that you understand us in a particular way. Hear our prayers and our petitions and plead for us in all our necessities, especially *(mention your request)*. May we be patient in learning God's Holy Will and courageous in carrying it out. Amen.

Saint Jude, pray for us! My Jesus, mercy!

Second Day

O blessed apostle Jude, who has been instrumental in gathering us here together this day, grant that we may always serve Jesus Christ as He deserves to be served, giving of our best efforts in living as He wishes us to live. May we dispose our hearts and minds that God will always be inclined to listen to our prayers and petitions, especially those petitions which we entrust to your care and for which we ask you to plead for us *(mention your request)*.

Grant that we may be enlightened as to what is best for us, in the present and future, not forgetting the blessings we have received in the past Amen.

Saint Jude, pray for us! My Jesus, mercy!

Third Day

O holy Saint Jude, apostle of Jesus Christ, you who have so faithfully and devotedly helped to spread His Gospel of Light, we who are gathered together today in your honor, ask and petition you to remember us and our needs. Especially do we pray for *(mention your request)*. May it also please our Lord to lend an ear to your supplications in our behalf. Grant that we may ever pray with fervor and devotion, resigning ourselves humbly to the Divine Will, seeing God's purpose in all our trials and knowing that He will leave no sincere prayer unanswered in some way. Amen.

Saint Jude, pray for us! My Jesus, mercy!

Fourth Day

Blessed Saint Jude, you were called to be one of Christ's chosen apostles and labored to bring men to a knowledge and love of God; listen with compassion to those gathered together to honor you and ask your intercession. In this troubled world of ours we have many trials, difficulties, and temptations. Plead for us in the heavenly court, asking that our petitions may be answered, especially the particular one we have in mind at this moment (*mention your request*). May it please God to answer our prayers in the way that He knows best, giving us grace to see His purpose in all things. Amen.

Saint Jude, pray for us! My Jesus, mercy!

Fifth Day

O holy Saint Jude, apostle and companion of Christ Jesus, you have shown us by example how to lead a life of zeal and devotion. We humbly entreat you today to hear our prayers and petitions.

Especially do we ask you to obtain for us the following favor (*mention your request*). Grant that in praying for present and future favors we may forget the innumerable ones granted in the past but often return to give thanks. Humbly we resign ourselves to God's holy Will, knowing that He alone knows what is best for us especially in our present needs and necessities. Amen.

Saint Jude, pray for us! My Jesus, mercy!

Sixth Day

Saint Jude, apostle of Christ and helper in despairing cases, hear the prayers and petitions of those who are gathered together in your honor. In all our needs and desires may we only seek what is pleasing to God and what is best for our salvation. These, our petitions *(mention your request)*, we submit to you, asking you to obtain them for us, if they are for the good of our souls. We are resigned to God's Holy Will in all things, knowing that He will leave no sincere prayer unanswered, though it may be in a way unexpected by us. Amen.

Saint Jude, pray for us! My Jesus, mercy!

Seventh Day

O holy apostle Saint Jude, in whose honor we are gathered today, may we never forget that our Lord and Savior Jesus Christ chose you to be one of the twelve apostles. Because of this and of the martyrdom you suffered for the Faith, we know you are a close friend of Almighty God. Therefore we do not hesitate to petition you in our necessities, especially *(mention your request)*. We humbly submit ourselves to the Will of God, knowing full well that no sincere prayer is ever left unanswered. May we see God's good and gracious purpose working in all our trials. Amen.

Saint Jude, pray for us! My Jesus, mercy!

Eighth Day

O holy Saint Jude, apostle of Christ, pray that we may ever imitate the Divine Master and live according to His Will. May we cooperate with the grace of God and ever remain pleasing in His sight.

Especially do we ask you to plead for us and obtain whatsoever is necessary for our salvation. Forget not our special petitions *(mention your request)*. May we always be thankful to God for the blessings we have received in the past Whatsoever we ask for the present or future, we submit to the Divine Will, realizing that God knows best what is good for us. We know He will respond to our prayers and petitions in one way or another. Amen.

Saint Jude, pray for us! My Jesus, mercy!

Ninth Day

O holy Saint Jude, apostle and martyr, grant that we may so dispose our lives that we may always be pleasing to God. In working out our salvation in this life we have many needs and necessities. Today we turn to you, asking you to intercede for us and obtain for us the favors we ask of God. Especially do we petition for *(mention your request)*.

May we not so much seek temporal good but rather what will avail our souls, knowing that it will profit us nothing if we gain the whole world yet suffer the loss of our soul.

Therefore, may we incline ourselves toward the divine will, seeing God's good and gracious purpose in all our trials. Amen.

Saint Jude, pray for us! My Jesus, mercy!

Infant of Prague Novena Prayer

O Jesus, Who has said, "Ask and you shall receive, seek and you shall find, knock and it shall be opened," through the intercession of Mary, Your Most Holy Mother, I knock, I seek, I ask that my prayer be granted.

(Mention your request.)

O Jesus, Who has said, "All that you ask of the Father in My Name, He will grant you," through the intercession of Mary Your Most Holy Mother, I humbly and urgently ask Your Father in Your Name that my prayer will be granted.

(Mention your request.)

O Jesus, Who has said, "Heaven and earth shall pass away but My word shall not pass away," through the intercession of Mary Your Most Holy Mother, I feel confident that my prayer will be granted.

(Mention your request.)

PRAYER OF THANKSGIVING

Divine Infant Jesus, I know You love me and would never leave me. I thank You for Your close Presence in my life.

Miraculous Infant, I believe in Your promise of peace, blessings, and freedom from want. I place every need and care in Your hands.

Lord Jesus, may I always trust in Your generous mercy and love. I want to honor and praise You, now and forever. Amen.

Infant of Prague Novena

First Day:

O! Sweet Child Jesus, here at Your feet is a soul that, conscious of its nothingness, turns to You, who are all. I have so much need of Your help. Look on me, O Jesus, with love, and since You are all powerful, help me in my poverty.

Our Father, Hail Mary, and Glory Be to the Father

Pray the following Prayer and Hymn daily:

By Your Divine Infancy, O Jesus, grant me the grace that I now ask (*mention your request*) if it is according to Your will and for my true good. Do not look upon my unworthiness, but rather on my faith and show me Your infinite mercy.

Hymn of the Most Holy Name of Jesus:

O Jesus, it is sweet to remember You, true joy of the heart,
but sweeter than honey,
than anything, is Your presence.
It is the most delightful song,
the most joyous to the ear;
it is the sweetest thought,
Jesus, Son of God.

Hope of the repentant,
benign with him who asks,
good with him who seeks,
how could one describe finding You?

The spoken word cannot describe,
nor the written word express,
only he who has experienced can believe
what it is to love Jesus.
O Jesus, be our joy and one day be our eternal rest;
in You is our glory
now and forever.
Amen.

Blessed be the name of the Lord. Now and forever. Amen.

Second Day

O Splendor of the heavenly Father, in whose face shines the light of the divinity, I adore You profoundly and I confess You as the true Son of the living God. I offer You, O Lord, the humble homage of all my being. Grant that I may never separate myself from You, my highest good.

Our Father, Hail Mary and Glory Be to the Father.

By Your Divine Infancy...

Third Day

O Holy Child Jesus, in gazing upon Your countenance, from which comes the most beautiful of smiles, I feel myself filled with a lively trust. Yes, I hope for all from Your goodness. Shed, O Jesus, on me and on those dear to me Your smile of grace, and I will praise Your infinite mercy.

Our Father, Hail Mary and Glory Be to the Father.

By Your Divine Infancy...

Fourth Day

O Child Jesus, whose forehead is adorned with a crown, I accept You as my absolute sovereign. I do not wish to serve any longer the evil one, my passions, or sin. Reign, O Jesus, over this poor heart and make it all Yours forever.

Our Father, Hail Mary, and Glory Be to the Father.

By Your Divine Infancy...

Fifth Day

I gaze upon You, O Most Sweet Redeemer, dressed in a mantle of purple. It is Your royal attire. How it speaks to me of blood, that Blood which You have shed solely on my account. Grant, O Child Jesus, that I may respond to Your great sacrifice and not refuse, when You offer me some difficulty, to suffer with You and for You.

Our Father, Hail Mary, and Glory Be to the Father.

By Your Divine Infancy...

Sixth Day

O Most Lovable Child, in contemplating You as You sustain the world, my heart fills with joy. Among the innumerable beings that You sustain I also am one. You look on me; uphold me at every instant and guard me as Your own. Look after, O Jesus, this humble being and help me in my many necessities.

Our Father, Hail Mary, and Glory Be to the Father.

By Your Divine Infancy...

Seventh Day

On Your breast, O Child Jesus, shines a Cross. It is the standard of our redemption. I also, O Divine Savior, have my cross, that, although light, very often weighs me down. Help me to bear it and may the carrying of it be fruitful. You well know how weak and worthless I am.

Our Father, Hail Mary, and Glory Be to the Father.

By Your Divine Infancy...

Eighth Day

Together with the cross, I see on Your breast, O Child Jesus, a little golden heart. It is the image of Your Heart, which is truly golden on account of Its infinite tenderness. You are the true friend, that generously gives Himself, even immolates Himself, for the one He loves. Continue to pour out on me, O Jesus, the enthusiasm which Your love inspires and teach me to respond always to Your great love.

Our Father, Hail Mary, and Glory Be to the Father.

By Your Divine Infancy...

Ninth Day

How many blessings, O Little Child, has Your Almighty right hand poured out on those who honor You and call upon You. Bless me also, O Child Jesus, my soul, my body, and my interests. Bless and help me in my necessities, and grant me what I now desire. Listen with compassion to my prayers and I will bless Your Holy Name every day.

Our Father, Hail Mary, and Glory Be to the Father.

By Your Divine Infancy...

Saint Gerard Novena:

Prayer for Motherhood

Good Saint Gerard, powerful intercessor before the throne of God, Wonder Worker of our day, I call upon you and seek your aid. You who on earth always fulfilled God's design, help me to do the Holy Will of God. Please ask the Master of life, from Whom all parenthood proceeds, to render me fruitful in offspring, that I may raise up children to God in this life and heirs to the Kingdom of His glory in the world to come. Amen.

Dear Mother Mary, please speak to Jesus for me. Amen.

Prayer for a Safe Delivery

O great Saint Gerard, beloved servant of Jesus Christ, perfect imitator of your meek and humble Savior, and devoted child of the Mother of God, enkindle within my heart one spark of that heavenly fire of charity which glowed in your heart and made you an angel of love.

O glorious Saint Gerard, because when falsely accused of crime, you did bear, like your Divine Master, without murmur or complaint, the calumnies of wicked men, you have been raised up by God as the patron and protector of expectant mothers.

Preserve me from danger and from the excessive pains accompanying childbirth, and shield the child which I now carry, that it may see the light of day and receive the purifying and life-giving waters of baptism, through Jesus Christ our Lord.

Amen.

Nine Days Novena to St Gerard Majella

Patron of Expecting Mothers

Please pray the following prayers for nine consecutive days:

Almighty and Eternal God,
we thank You for the gift of Saint Gerard
and the example of his life.
Because Saint Gerard always had complete faith and trust in You,
You blessed him with great powers of help and healing.
Through him, You showed your loving concern
for all those who suffered or were in need.
You never failed to hear his prayer on their behalf.
Today, through Saint Gerard's powerful intercession,
You continue to show your love
for all those who place their trust in You.
And so, Father, full of faith and confidence,
and in thanksgiving for all the wonderful things
You have done for us,
we place ourselves before You today.
Through the intercession of Saint Gerard,
hear our prayers and petitions,
and if it is Your Holy Will,
please grant them in the name of Jesus, Our Lord.

Amen.

First Day

Saint Gerard, ever full of faith, obtain for me that, believing firmly all that the Church of God proposes to my belief, I may strive to secure through a holy life, the joys of eternal happiness. *Pray nine Hail Marys.*

Second Day

Saint Gerard, most generous saint, who from your earliest years did care so little for the goods of earth, grant that I may place all my confidence in Jesus Christ alone, my true Treasure, who alone can make me happy in time and eternity. *Pray nine Hail Marys.*

Third Day

Saint Gerard, bright seraph of love, who despising all earthly love, consecrated your life to the service of God and your neighbor, promoting God's glory in your lowly state, and ever ready to assist the distressed and console the sorrowful, obtain for me, I beg you, that loving God, the only good, and my neighbor for His sake, I may be hereafter united to Him forever in glory. *Pray nine Hail Marys.*

Fourth Day

Saint Gerard, spotless lily of purity, by the angelic virtue and wonderful innocence of your life you received from the Infant Jesus and His Immaculate Mother, sweet pledges of tender love.

Grant, I beg you, that I may ever strive courageously in my lifelong fight, and therefore win the crown that awaits the brave and the true. *Pray nine Hail Marys.*

Fifth Day

Saint Gerard, model of holy obedience, throughout your life you heroically submitted your judgment to those who represented Jesus Christ to you, thereby sanctifying your lowliest actions.

Please obtain for me from God cheerful submission to His Holy Will and the virtue of perfect obedience, that I may be made conformable to Jesus, my Model, who was obedient even to death. *Pray nine Hail Marys.*

Sixth Day

Saint Gerard, most perfect imitator of Jesus Our Redeemer, your greatest glory was to be humble and lowly.

Please obtain that I too, knowing my littleness in God's sight, may be found worthy to enter the kingdom that is promised to the humble and lowly of heart. *Pray nine Hail Marys.*

Seventh Day

Saint Gerard, unconquered hero, most patient in suffering, you who did glory in infirmity, and under slander and most cruel ignominy did rejoice to suffer with Christ, obtain for me patience and resignation in my sorrows, that I may bravely bear the cross that is to gain for me the crown of everlasting glory. *Pray nine Hail Marys.*

Eighth Day

Saint Gerard, true lover of Jesus in the Blessed Sacrament of the Altar, you who knelt long hours before the Tabernacle, and there tasted the joys of paradise; obtain for me an undying love for the Most Holy Sacrament, that receiving frequently the Body and Blood of Jesus, I may daily grow in His holy love and merit the priceless grace of loving Him even to the end. *Pray nine Hail Marys.*

Ninth Day

Saint Gerard, most favored child of heaven, to whom Mary gave the Infant Jesus in the days of your childhood, and to whom she sweetly came before you closed your eyes in death; obtain for me I beseech you, so to seek and love my Blessed Mother during life, that she may be my joy and consolation in this valley of tears, until with you, before the throne of God, I may praise her goodness for all eternity.

Amen.

Pray nine Hail Marys.

Novena to the Holy Spirit

Every day begin by praying the following prayer:

O Holy Spirit, divine Consoler!
I adore you as my True God.
I bless You by uniting myself to the praises
You receive from the angel and saints.
I offer You my whole heart,
and I render You heartfelt thanks
for all the benefits You have bestowed
and do unceasingly bestow upon the world.
I beg You, Who are the Author of all supernatural gifts
And Who enriched with immense favors the soul
of the Blessed Virgin Mary,
the Mother of God,
to visit me by Your grace and Your love,
and grant me the favor
I so earnestly seek in this novena...*(Mention your request).*
O Holy Spirit,
Spirit of truth,
come into our hearts:
shed the brightness of Your light on all nations,
that they may be of one faith and pleasing to You.

Amen.

Come, O Holy Spirit,
fill the hearts of your faithful,
and kindle in them the fire of Your love.

First Day

O Holy Spirit,
bestow upon us Your seven holy gifts.
Enlighten our understanding that we may know You.
Give us wisdom that Your will may be clear to us
and that we may accept it.
Grant us the gift of counsel
that we may always perceive what is right.
Fortify us that we may always be capable
of fulfilling Your Divine Will.
Inspire us with the spirit of learning
that we may be able to penetrate more deeply
into the truths that You have revealed.
Let our hearts be steeped in the spirit of childlikeness
that we may bring You joy.
Let us have proper fear of God
that we may never grieve You
or wander from the path of goodness.
Give us the fullness of Your gifts
that we may glorify You.

Amen.

Second Day

O Holy Spirit,

make me faithful in every thought,

and grant that I may always listen to Your voice,

watch for Your light,

and follow Your gracious inspirations.

I cling to You,

give myself to You,

and ask You by Your compassion

to watch over me in my weakness.

Holding the pierced feet of Jesus,

looking at His Five Wounds,

trusting in His Precious Blood,

adoring His opened side and stricken Heart,

I implore You, adorable Spirit,

helper of my infirmity,

to keep me in Your grace,

now and always,

Amen.

Third Day

Heavenly Father, You have called me to be a member of the Mystical Body of Your Son, Jesus Christ, and to be a temple of the Holy Spirit.

I ask You to give me Wisdom, that I may understand the follies of this world; Understanding, that I may grasp more fully the meaning of my existence and the purpose of all things in the world; Counsel, that I may always choose the proper way; Fortitude, that I may remain faithful to You under the pressure of temptation; Piety, that I may revere You in all I do, think, or say; Fear of the Lord, that should the motive of love fail me, I may quickly be awakened to the eternal consequences of my deeds.

Visit me by Your grace and Your love.

Amen.

Fourth Day

O God, by the light of Your Holy Spirit, give us a love for what is right and just and a constant enjoyment of His comforts.

O Holy Spirit, may we always know the wonder of God Who is beyond all our imagination.

Pray that I may accept as the motto of my life:

"All for the greater glory of God."

Amen.

Fifth Day

Come, O Spirit of sanctity,
and send forth the radiance of Your light.
Father of all the poor,
light and peace of all hearts,
come with Your countless gifts.
Consoler in desolation,
refreshment full of loveliness,
come dear Friend of my soul.
In weariness send repose;
breathe gently cool refreshing breeze;
console the desolate who weep alone.
Light of Beatitude,
make our hearts ready;
come enter our souls.
Without Your grace,
we stand alone;
we cannot be good or sure.
Cleanse what is soiled;
heal what is wounded;
moisten what is arid.
Bend the stubborn will;
warm the cold heart;
and guide the wandering footstep. Amen.

Sixth Day

O Father in Heaven, may Your Holy Spirit remind me of Your love, Your promises, Your sanctity, omniscience, wisdom, goodness, faithfulness, and love. May Your Holy Spirit encourage me when I am slothful; strengthen me when I am weak; and enlighten me when I no longer can help myself.

Breathe into me, O Holy Spirit, that I may do what is holy. Stir me, that I may love what is holy. Strengthen me, that I may preserve what is holy. Protect me, Holy Spirit, that I may never lose what is holy.

Amen.

Seventh Day

Come, Holy Spirit, creator of all things: come visit our hearts with Your power.

Fill with grace, friendly guest, the hearts which You have created.

You are called the Consoler, gift from the hand of God, source of life, light, love, and flame, highest good.

You are the pledge of sevenfold grace, finger of the Father's hand,

promised us by Him, and You make our tongues speak the truth.

Cast light on our senses, pour love into our hearts.

Grant our weak bodies strength that they may never grow weary of doing good.

Keep the enemy far from us, give us peace always, and let us willingly follow in Your footsteps that we may be far removed from sin.

Grant that through You we may grow in knowledge of the Father and of the Son, and that we may ever strongly believe in You, the Spirit of both.

Praise and honor be forever to the Father on the highest throne, in the risen Son of God, in the Consoler.

Amen.

Eighth Day

O Holy Spirit, life and light of the Church, give us thoughts higher than our own thoughts, prayers better than our own prayers, and powers beyond our own powers, that we may love and live, imitating Jesus Christ, our Lord and Savior.

Come to us, Holy Spirit, come with the Father and the Son.

Dwell within our souls and quickly make our hearts Your own.

Quench in us the fires of hate and strife, the wasting fever of the heart.

From perils guard our feeble life and to our souls Your peace impart.

Let voice and mind and heart and strength confess and glorify Your name and let the fire of charity burn bright and other hearts inflame.

Amen.

Ninth Day

O Lord, Holy Spirit, grant me sight to see the wondrous promise of divine love, insight to see my own weakness, and delight in Your divine presence in my soul which You have made Your temple through sanctifying grace.

I pray, O Holy Spirit, that I may be not doubting, that I be spared the pain of being alone without trust or hope in Christ, and that my prayer may always be "My Lord and my God!"

I pray that I may acquire a sense of retreat to prayer and recollection at various times in my daily life; for prayer is the bond that joins us to Christ.

I pray that I may be aware of the physical needs of the poor and that I may share what I can with them in the charitable works of the Church.

I pray, O Holy Spirit, that You will in Your mercy grant me the favor I have sought in this novena.

Amen.

In times of need we can follow the example of Our Lord, and flee to the protection of His, and our, Blessed Mother.

Pray the following prayers each day for nine days:

Novena to Our Lady of Perpetual Help

Mother of Perpetual Help, behold at your feet a sinner who has recourse to you and has confidence in you. Mother of mercy, have pity on me. I hear all calling you the refuge and hope of sinners. Be, then, my refuge and my hope. For the love of Jesus Christ, your Son, help me.

Give your hand to a poor sinner who commends himself (herself) to you and dedicates himself (herself) to your lasting service. I praise and thank God, Who, in His mercy, has given to me this confidence in you, a sure pledge of my eternal salvation.

It is true that in the past, miserable and wretched, I have fallen into sin because I did not have recourse to you. But I know that with your help, I shall be able to overcome myself. I know, too, that you will help me, if I commend myself to you. But I fear that in the occasions of sin, I may neglect to call upon you and thus run the risk of being lost.

This grace, then, I seek of you; for this I implore you as much as I can: that in all the attacks of hell I may ever have recourse to you and say to you: "O Mary, help me. O Mother of Perpetual Help, do not let me lose my God."

Three Hail Marys.

Our Lady of Perpetual Help Novena

Mother of Perpetual Help, aid me ever to call upon your powerful name, since your name is the help of the living and the salvation of the dying. Mary most pure, Mary most sweet, grant that your name from this day forth, may be to me the very breath of life. Dear Lady, do not delay in coming to help me when I call upon you, for in all the temptations that trouble me, in all the needs of my life, I will ever call upon you, repeating: "Mary, Mary."

What comfort, what sweetness, what confidence, what consolation fills my soul at the sound of your name, at the very thought of you! I give thanks to our Lord, Who for my sake has given you a name so sweet, so lovable, and so mighty. But I am not content only to speak your name; I will call upon you because I love you. I want that love to remind me always to call you Mother of Perpetual Help.

Three Hail Marys.

Novena Prayer to Our Lady of Perpetual Help

Mother of Perpetual Help, you are the dispenser of every grace that God grants us in our misery. For this reason, He has made you so powerful, so rich, and so kind, that you might help us in our needs.

You are the advocate of the most wretched and abandoned sinners, if they but come to you. Come to my aid, for I commend myself to you.

In your hands I place my eternal salvation; to you I entrust my soul.

Count me among your most faithful servants. Take me under your protection; that is enough for me. If you protect me, I shall fear nothing: not my sins, because you are mightier than the powers of hell; not even Jesus, my Judge, because He is appeased by a single prayer of yours.

I fear only that through my own negligence I may forget to recommend myself to you, and so lose my soul. My dear Lady, obtain for me the forgiveness of my sins, love for Jesus, final perseverance, and the grace to have recourse to you at all times, Mother of Perpetual Help.

Three Hail Marys.

– composed by Saint Alphonsus Liguori

Novena to Saint Peregrine

Saint Peregrine Laziosi was born in 1260 at Forli, Italy, where he enjoyed an affluent life. After his conversion, he gave his life to God, eventually joining the Servite Order. Saint Peregrine dedicated his life to caring for the sick, poor, and marginalized. At age 60, he was diagnosed with a severe cancer of the leg.

The night before his leg was to be amputated, Saint Peregrine dragged himself before the crucifix and begged the crucified Lord to heal him. Falling into a deep trance-like sleep, he saw Jesus lean down from the Cross to touch his leg. He awoke the following morning completely healed! Saint Peregrine is invoked for healing of many serious diseases, especially cancer.

Saint Peregrine Novena

Pray the following prayers daily for nine days:

O God, who gave to Saint Peregrine an Angel for his companion, the Mother of God for his Teacher, and Jesus as the Physician of his malady, grant we beseech You through his merits that we may on earth intensely love our Holy Angel, the blessed Virgin Mary, and our Savior, and in Him bless them forever. Grant that we may receive the favor for which we now petition. We ask this through the same Christ our Lord. Amen.

Seven Our Fathers, Seven Hail Marys and Seven Glory Be to the Fathers with the invocation "Saint Peregrine, pray for us."

Saint Peregrine Novena Prayer

O Glorious wonder worker, Saint Peregrine, you answered the divine call with a ready spirit, and forsook all the comforts of a life of ease and all the empty honors of the world to dedicate yourself to God in the Order of His holy Mother. You labored manfully for the salvation of souls. In union with Jesus crucified, you endured painful sufferings with such patience as to deserve to be healed miraculously of an incurable cancer in your leg by a touch of His divine hand. Obtain for me the grace to answer every call of God and to fulfill His will in all the events of life. Enkindle in my heart a consuming zeal for the salvation of all men. Deliver me from the infirmities that afflict my body *(especially...)*. Obtain for me also a perfect resignation to the sufferings it may please God to send me, so that, imitating our crucified Savior and His sorrowful Mother, I may merit eternal glory in heaven.

Saint Peregrine, pray for me and for all who invoke your aid.

Prayer to Saint Peregrine

Oh great Saint Peregrine, you have been called "The Mighty" and "The Wonder Worker" because of the numerous miracles which you have obtained from God for those who have had recourse to you. For many years you bore in your own flesh this cancerous disease that destroys the very fiber of our being, and you had recourse to the source of all grace when the power of man could do no more. You were favored with the vision of Jesus coming down from His Cross to heal your affliction. Ask of God and Our Lady, the cure of these sick persons whom we entrust to you.

Aided in this way by your powerful intercession, we shall sing to God, now and for all eternity, a song of gratitude for His great goodness and mercy. Amen.

Novena to Our Lady Of The Miraculous Medal

Pray the following prayers daily for nine days:

Come Holy Spirit, fill the hearts of Your faithful and kindle in them the fire of Your love. Send forth Your Spirit, and they shall be created.

And You shall renew the face of the earth.

Let us pray. O God, Who has instructed the hearts of the faithful by the light of the Holy Spirit, grant us in the same Spirit to be truly wise, and ever to rejoice in His consolation. Through Jesus Christ our Lord.

Amen.

O Mary, conceived without sin,

Pray for us who have recourse to you. *(Three times)*

Lord Jesus Christ, Who has glorified Your Mother, the Blessed Virgin Mary, immaculate from the first moment of her conception, grant that all who devoutly implore her protection on earth may eternally enjoy Your presence in heaven. Lord Jesus Christ, Who for the accomplishment of Your greatest works has chosen the weak things of the world, that no flesh may glory in Your sight, and Who for a better and more widely diffused belief in the Immaculate Conception of Your Mother, has wished that the Miraculous Medal be manifested to Saint Catherine Laboure, grant, we ask You that filled with like humility, we may glorify this mystery by word and work.

Amen.

Memorare

Remember, O most gracious Virgin Mary, that never was it known, that anyone who fled to your protection, implored your assistance, or sought your intercession, was left unaided. Inspired with this confidence, I fly unto you, O Virgin of Virgins, my Mother; to you I come; before you I kneel, sinful and sorrowful. O Mother of the Word Incarnate, despise not my petitions, but in your mercy hear and answer them.

Amen.

Novena Prayer

Immaculate Virgin Mary, mother of our Lord Jesus and our mother, we have confidence in your powerful and never-failing intercession, manifested so often through the Miraculous Medal. We, your loving and trustful children, ask you to obtain for us the graces and favors we ask during this novena if they will be for the glory of God and the salvation of souls. *(Mention your request)*.

You know, O Mary, how often our souls have been the sanctuaries of your Son, who hates iniquity. Obtain for us then a deep hatred of sin and that purity of heart which will attach us to God alone so that our every thought, word, and deed may tend to His greater glory.

Obtain for us also a spirit of prayer and self-denial that we may recover by penance what we have lost by sin and at length attain to that blessed abode where you are the Queen of angels and of men.

Amen.

Prayer to Our Lady of the Miraculous Medal

O Virgin Mother of God, Mary Immaculate, we unite ourselves to you under your title of Our Lady of the Miraculous Medal. May this medal be for each one of us a sure sign of your motherly affection for us and a constant reminder of our filial duties toward you. While wearing it, may we be blessed by your loving protection and preserved in the grace of your Son. Most powerful Virgin, Mother of our Savior, keep us close to you every moment of our lives so that, like you, we may live and act according to the teaching and example of your Son. Obtain for us, your children, the grace of a happy death so that in union with you we may enjoy the happiness of heaven forever. Amen.

O Mary, conceived without sin,

Pray for us who have recourse to you.

Closing Prayer

O Mary conceived without sin, pray for us:

O Mary conceived without sin, pray for us who have recourse to thee.

Pray the following prayers daily for nine days:

Novena Prayer in Honor of Saint Dymphna

Patron Saint of Family Harmony, Mental Illness, and the Emotionally Disturbed

Lord, our God, You graciously chose Saint Dymphna as patroness of those afflicted with mental and nervous disorders.

She is thus an inspiration and a symbol of charity to the thousands who ask her intercession.

Please grant, Lord, through the prayers of this pure youthful martyr, relief and consolation to all suffering such trials, and especially those for whom we pray.

(Mention those for whom you wish to pray.)

We beg You, Lord, to hear the prayers of Saint Dymphna on our behalf.

Grant all those for whom we pray patience in their sufferings and resignation to Your Divine Will.

Please fill them with hope, and grant them the relief and cure they so much desire.

We ask this through Christ our Lord, Who suffered agony in the garden.

Amen.

Saint Dymphna Novena

Saint Dymphna, a great wonder worker in every affliction of mind and body, I humbly implore your powerful intercession with Jesus through Mary, the Health of the Sick.

You are filled with love and compassion for the thousands of patients brought to your shrine for centuries and for those who cannot come to your shrine but invoke you in their homes or in hospitals. Show the same love and compassion toward me, your faithful client. The many miracles you have wrought through your intercession give me great confidence that you will help me in my present need. *(Mention your request)*.

I am confident of obtaining my request, if it is for the greater glory of God and the good of my soul. For the sake of Jesus and Mary, whom you loved so earnestly, and for whom you offered your life in martyrdom, grant my prayer.

St Dymphna, young and beautiful, innocent and pure, help me to imitate your love of purity. You chose to be martyred by your own father's sword rather than consent to sin. Give me strength and courage in fighting off the temptations of the world and evil desires.

As you have given all the love of your heart to Jesus, help me to love God with my whole heart and serve Him faithfully. As you bore the persecution of your father and the sufferings of an exile so patiently, obtain for me the patience I need to accept the trials of my life with loving resignation to the Will of God.

Our Lady of Mt. Carmel Novena

First Day

O Beautiful Flower of Carmel, most fruitful vine, splendor of heaven, holy and singular, who brought forth the Son of God, still ever remaining a pure virgin, assist us in our necessity! O Star of the Sea, help and protect us! Show us that you are our Mother! *(Pause and mention petitions.)*

Our Lady of Mount Carmel, pray for us.

Second Day

Most Holy Mary, Our Mother, in your great love for us you gave us the Holy Scapular of Mount Carmel, having heard the prayers of your chosen son Saint Simon Stock. Help us now to wear it faithfully and with devotion. May it be a sign to us of our desire to grow in holiness. *(Pause and mention petitions.)*

Our Lady of Mount Carmel, pray for us.

Third Day

O Queen of Heaven, you gave us the Scapular as an outward sign by which we might be known as your faithful children. May we always wear it with honor by avoiding sin and imitating your virtues. Help us to be faithful to this desire of ours. *(Pause and mention petitions.)*

Our Lady of Mount Carmel, pray for us.

One Our Father, Hail Mary, and Glory Be to the Father at the end of each day's prayers.

Fourth Day

When you gave us, Gracious Lady, the Scapular as our Habit, you called us to be not only servants, but also your own children.

We ask you to gain for us from your Son the grace to live as your children in joy, peace and love. *(Pause and mention petitions.)*

Our Lady of Mount Carmel, pray for us.

Fifth Day

O Mother of Fair Love, through your goodness, as your children, we are called to live in the spirit of Carmel. Help us to live in charity with one another, prayerful as Elijah of old, and mindful of our call to minister to God's people. *(Pause and mention petitions.)*

Our Lady of Mount Carmel, pray for us.

Sixth Day

With loving provident care, O Mother Most Amiable, you covered us with your Scapular as a shield of defense against the Evil One.

Through your assistance, may we bravely struggle against the powers of evil, always open to your Son, Jesus Christ. *(Pause and mention petitions.)*

Our Lady of Mount Carmel, pray for us.

One Our Father, Hail Mary, and Glory Be to the Father at the end of each day's prayers.

Seventh Day

O Mary, Help of Christians, you assured us that wearing your Scapular worthily would keep us safe from harm. Protect us in both body and soul with your continual aid. May all that we do be pleasing to your Son and to you. *(Pause and mention petitions.)*

Our Lady of Mount Carmel, pray for us.

One Our Father, Hail Mary, and Glory Be to the Father.

Eighth Day

You give us hope, O Mother of Mercy, that through your Scapular promise we might quickly pass through the fires of purgatory to the Kingdom of your Son. Be our comfort and our hope.

Grant that our hope may not be in vain but that, ever faithful to your Son and to you, we may speedily enjoy after death the blessed company of Jesus and the saints. *(Pause and mention petitions.)*

Our Lady of Mount Carmel, pray for us.

One Our Father, Hail Mary, and Glory Be to the Father.

Ninth Day

O Most Holy Mother of Mount Carmel, when asked by a saint to grant privileges to the family of Carmel, you gave assurance of your Motherly love and help to those faithful to you and to your Son.

Behold us, your children. We glory in wearing your holy habit, which makes us members of your family of Carmel, through which we shall have your powerful protection in life, at death, and even after death.

Look down with love, O Gate of Heaven, on all those now in their last agony!

Look down graciously, O Virgin, Flower of Carmel, on all those in need of help!

Look down mercifully, O Mother of our Savior, on all those who do not know that they are numbered among your children.

Look down tenderly, O Queen of All Saints, on the poor souls! *(Pause and mention petitions.)*

Our Lady of Mount Carmel, pray for us.

One Our Father, Hail Mary, and Glory Be to the Father.

Saint Rita of Cascia

Saint Rita was born at Spoleto, Italy, in 1381. From her early youth, Rita felt a call to the consecrated life, and she begged her parents for permission to enter the convent. However, when she was twelve, they betrothed her to the town watchman, a man who struggled with a violent temper. Rita obediently married him and bore twin sons.

Rita put up with her husband's mistreatment as best she could, praying and receiving the sacraments frequently. Unfortunately, her sons learned from their father's violent ways. After eighteen years of marriage, her husband was stabbed to death by an enemy, but repented on his deathbed, thanks to Rita's prayers. Rita's sons were determined to avenge their father, but through Rita's prayers, they forgave his murderers, and shortly thereafter died themselves.

After some delay, Rita was admitted to the Augustinian monastery of Saint Magdalen at age 36. She lived 40 years in the convent, in great prayer and charity, working for peace in the area. She had a great devotion to the Passion of Christ, and begged to suffer as He had. One day, a thorn from the crucifix pierced her forehead, causing a deep wound which did not heal. After suffering 15 years, Saint Rita died of tuberculosis on May 22, 1457.

Saint Rita is well known as a patron of desperate, seemingly impossible causes and situations. This is because she was involved in so many stages of life - wife, mother, widow, and nun.

Novena Prayer to Saint Rita, Patroness of Impossible Causes

O Holy Patroness of those in need, Saint Rita, whose pleadings before thy Divine Lord are almost irresistible, who for thy lavishness in granting favors has been called the Advocate of the hopeless and even of the impossible; Saint Rita, so humble, so pure, so mortified, so patient, and of such compassionate love for your Crucified Jesus that you could obtain from Him whatsoever you ask, on account of which all confidently have recourse to you expecting, if not always relief, at least comfort; be propitious to our petition, showing your power with God on behalf of your suppliant; be lavish to us, as you have been in so many wonderful cases, for the greater glory of God, for the spreading of your own devotion, and for the consolation of those who trust in you.

We promise, if our petition is granted, to glorify you by making known your favor, to bless and sing your praises forever. Relying then upon your merits and power before the Sacred Heart of Jesus, we pray you grant that ... *(Mention your request)*.

By the singular merits of your childhood,
By your perfect union with the Divine Will,
By your heroic sufferings during your married life,
By the consolation you experienced at the conversion of your husband,
By the sacrifice of your children rather than see them grievously offend God,
By your miraculous entrance into the convent,
By your severe penances,
By the suffering caused by the wound you received from the thorn of your Crucified Savior,
By the Divine Love which consumed your heart,
By that remarkable devotion to the Blessed Sacrament, on which alone you existed for four years,
By the happiness with which you parted from your trials to join your Divine Spouse,
By the perfect example you gave to people of every state of life,
Pray for us, O holy Saint Rita, that we may be made worthy of the promises of Christ.

Let us pray

O God, Who in Your infinite tenderness has regarded the prayer of Your servant, Blessed Rita, and has granted to her supplication that which is impossible to human foresight, skill, and efforts, in reward of her compassionate love and firm reliance on Your promise, have pity on our adversity and help us in our calamities, that the unbeliever may know You are the recompense of the humble, the defense of the helpless, and the strength of those who trust in You, through Jesus Christ, Our Lord.

Amen.

Novena to Saint Anne

Mother of the Virgin Mary and
Grandmother of Jesus

Pray this prayer daily:

Glorious Saint Anne,

filled with compassion for those who invoke you,

with love for those who suffer,

heavily laden with the weight of my troubles,

I kneel at your feet and humbly beg you

to take my present need under your special protection...

(State your intention here.)

Please recommend it to your daughter,

the Blessed Virgin Mary,

and lay it before the throne of Jesus.

Cease not to intercede for me until my request is granted.

Above all, obtain for me the grace to one day meet God face to

face, and with you and Mary, and all the angels

and saints, to praise Him through all eternity. Amen.

First Day

Great Saint Anne, engrave indelibly on my heart and in my mind the words that have reclaimed and sanctified so many sinners: "What shall it profit a man to gain the whole world if he lose his own soul?"

May this be the principle fruit of these prayers by which I will strive to honor you during this novena.

At your feet I renew my resolution to invoke you daily, not only for the success of my temporal affairs and to be preserved from sickness and suffering, but above all, that I may be preserved from all sin, that I may succeed in working out my eternal salvation and that I will receive the special grace of... *(State your intention here.)*

O most powerful Saint Anne, do not let me lose my soul, but obtain for me the grace of winning my way to heaven, there with you, your blessed spouse, and your glorious daughter, to sing the praise of the most holy and adorable Trinity forever and ever.

Amen.

Our Father...

Hail Mary...

Glory Be to the Father...

Pray for us, Saint Anne!

That we may be made worthy of the promises of Christ.

Second Day

Glorious Saint Anne, how can you be otherwise than overflowing with tenderness toward sinners like myself, since you are the grandmother of Him who shed His blood for them, and the mother of her whom the saints call advocate of sinners?

To you, therefore, I address my prayers with confidence.

Please commend me to Jesus and Mary so that, at your request, I may be granted remission of my sins, perseverance, the love of God, charity for all mankind, and the special grace of... *(state your intention here)* which I stand in need of at the present time.

O most powerful protectress, let me not lose my soul, but obtain for me that through the merits of Jesus Christ and the intercession of Mary, I may have the happiness of seeing them, of loving and praising them with you through all eternity. Amen.

Our Father...

Hail Mary...

Glory Be to the Father...

Pray for us, Saint Anne!

That we may be made worthy of the promises of Christ.

Third Day

Beloved of Jesus, Mary, and Joseph, mother of the Queen of Heaven, take us and all who are dear to us under your special care.

Obtain for us the virtues you instilled in the heart of her who was destined to become Mother of God, and the graces with which you were endowed.

Sublime model of Christian womanhood, pray that we may imitate your example in our homes and families, listen to our petitions, and obtain our request of... *(State your intention here.)*

Guardian of the infancy and childhood of the most Blessed Virgin Mary, obtain the graces necessary for all who enter the marriage state, that imitating your virtues they may sanctify their homes and lead the souls entrusted to their care to eternal glory.

Amen.

Our Father...

Hail Mary...

Glory Be to the Father...

Pray for us, Saint Anne!

That we may be made worthy of the promises of Christ.

Fourth Day

Glorious Saint Anne, I kneel in confidence at your feet, for you also have tasted the bitterness and sorrow of life.

My necessities, the cause of my tears, are... *(State your intention here.)*

Good Saint Anne, you who did suffer much during the years that preceded your glorious maternity, I beseech you, by all your sufferings and humiliations, to grant my prayer.

I pray to you, through your love for your glorious spouse Saint Joachim, through your love for your immaculate child, through the joy you felt at the moment of her happy birth, not to refuse me.

Bless me, bless my family and all who are dear to me, so that some day we may all be with you in the glory of heaven, for all eternity.

Amen.

Our Father...

Hail Mary...

Glory Be to the Father...

Pray for us, Saint Anne!

That we may be made worthy of the promises of Christ.

Fifth Day

Great Saint Anne, how far I am from resembling you.

I so easily give way to impatience and discouragement; and so easily give up praying when God does not at once answer my request.

Prayer is the key to all heavenly treasures and I cannot pray, because my weak faith and lack of confidence fail me at the slightest delay of Divine Mercy.

O my powerful protectress, come to my aid, listen to my petition... *(State your intention here.)*

Make my confidence and fervor, supported by the promise of Jesus Christ, redouble in proportion as the trial to which God in His goodness subjects me is prolonged, that I may obtain like you more than I can venture to ask for.

In the future I will remember that I am made for heaven and not for earth; for eternity and not for time; that consequently I must ask, above all, the salvation of my soul which is assured to all who pray properly and who persevere in prayer.

Amen.

Our Father...

Hail Mary...

Glory Be to the Father...

Pray for us, Saint Anne!

That we may be made worthy of the promises of Christ.

Sixth Day

Glorious Saint Anne, mother of the Mother of God, I beg you to obtain through your powerful intercession the pardon of my sins and the assistance I need in my troubles... *(State your intention here.)*

What can I not hope for if you condescend to take me under your protection?

The Most High has been pleased to grant the prayers of sinners, whenever you have been charitable enough to be their advocate.

Kneeling at your feet, I beg you to help me in all spiritual and temporal dangers; to guide me in the true path of Christian perfection, and finally to obtain for me the grace of ending my life with the death of the just, so that I may contemplate face to face your beloved Jesus and daughter Mary in your loving companionship throughout eternity.

Amen.

Our Father...

Hail Mary...

Glory Be to the Father...

Pray for us, Saint Anne!

That we may be made worthy of the promises of Christ.

Seventh Day

O Good Saint Anne, so justly called the mother of the infirm and the cure for those who suffer from disease, look kindly upon the sick for whom I pray; alleviate their sufferings; and cause them to sanctify their sufferings by patience and complete submission to the Divine Will.

Finally dear Saint Anne, please obtain health for them and with it the firm resolution to honor Jesus, Mary, and yourself by the faithful performance of duties.

But, merciful Saint Anne, I ask you above all for the salvation of my soul, rather than bodily health, for I am convinced that this fleeting life is given us solely to assure us a better one.

Now, we cannot obtain that better life without the help of God's graces.

I earnestly beg them of you for the sick and for myself, especially for the petition which I am making in this novena... *(state your intention here)* through the merits of our Lord Jesus Christ, through the intercession of His Immaculate Mother, and through your efficacious and powerful mediation.

O glorious Saint Anne, Amen.

Our Father...

Hail Mary...

Glory Be to the Father...

Pray for us, Saint Anne!

That we may be made worthy of the promises of Christ.

Eighth Day

Remember, O Saint Anne, you whose name signifies grace and mercy, that never was it known that anyone who fled to your protection, implored your help, and sought your intercession was left unaided.

Inspired with this confidence, I fly unto you, good and kind mother; I take refuge at your feet, burdened with the weight of my sins.

O holy mother of the Immaculate Virgin Mary, despise not my petition... *(state your intention here)* but hear me and grant my prayer.

Amen.

Our Father...

Hail Mary...

Glory Be to the Father...

Pray for us, Saint Anne!

That we may be made worthy of the promises of Christ.

Ninth Day

Most holy mother of the Virgin Mary, glorious Saint Anne, I, a miserable sinner, confiding in your kindness, choose you today as my special advocate.

I offer and consecrate my person and all my interests to your care and maternal solicitude.

I hope to serve you and honor you all my life for the love of your most holy daughter and to do all in my power to spread devotion to you.

O my very good mother and advocate, be pleased to accept me as your servant, and to adopt me as your child.

O glorious Saint Anne, I beg you, by the passion of my most loving Jesus, the Son of Mary, your most holy daughter, to assist me in all the necessities both of my body and my soul.

Venerable Mother, I beg you to obtain for me the favor I seek in this novena... *(state your intention here)* and the grace of leading a life perfectly conformable in all things to the Divine Will.

I place my soul in your hands and in those of your kind daughter.

I confide it to you, above all at the moment when it will be separated from my body, in order that, appearing under your patronage before the Supreme Judge, He may find it worthy of enjoying His Divine Presence in your holy companionship in Heaven.

Amen.

Our Father...

Hail Mary...

Glory Be to the Father...

Pray for us, Saint Anne!

That we may be made worthy of the promises of Christ.